I See Stars

D.H. Dilkes

Bailey Books
an imprint of
Enslow Publishers, Inc.
40 Industrial Road
Box 398
Berkeley Heights, NJ 07922
USA
http://www.enslow.com

Bailey Books, an imprint of Enslow Publishers, Inc.

Copyright © 2011 by Enslow Publishers, Inc.

Library of Congress Cataloging-in-Publication Data

Dilkes, D. H.
  I see stars / by D.H. Dilkes.
    p. cm. — (All about shapes)
  Includes index.
  Summary: "Simple text and photographs present a story with a theme about stars"—
Provided by publisher.
  ISBN 978-0-7660-3803-5
  1. Stars (Shape)—Juvenile literature. 2. Shapes—Juvenile literature. I. Title.
  QA482.D538 2011
  516'.154—dc22
                              2010018404

Paperback ISBN: 978-1-59845-154-2

Printed in the United States of America

052010 Lake Book Manufacturing, Inc., Melrose Park, IL

10 9 8 7 6 5 4 3 2 1

Photo Credits: Shutterstock.com

Cover Photo: Shutterstock.com

Note to Parents and Teachers

Help pre-readers get a jumpstart on reading. These lively stories introduce simple concepts
with repetition of words and short simple sentences. Photos and illustrations fill the pages
with color and effectively enhance the text. Free Educator Guides are available for this series
at www.enslow.com. Search for the *All About Shapes* series name.

Contents

Words to Know

  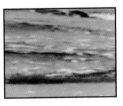

star   tree   water

I see stars.

Some we fly.

One by the water,

one we can try.

**This is fun
to draw.**

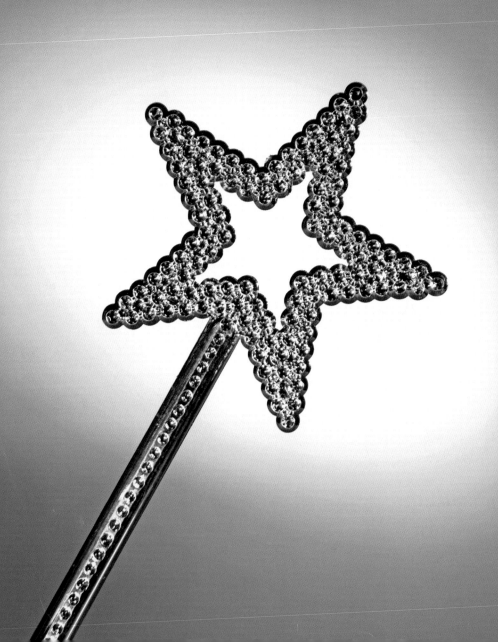

This my sister saw.

A star I can eat.

Star on the
street.

One on a tree.

One looks good on me!

Read More

Olson, Nathan. *Stars Around Town.* Mankato, Minn.: Capstone Press, 2007.

Rau, Dana Meachen. *A Star in My Orange: Looking for Nature's Shapes.* Brookfield, Conn.: Millbrook Press, 2002.

Web Sites

Fisher-Price. *Learn Your Colors and Shapes.*
<http://www.fisher-price.com/us/fun/games/colorshapes>
Press any key to start!

nickjr. Dora's Star-Catching Storybook.
<http://www.nickjr.com/printables/star-catching-storybook.jhtml>
Read, print, and color!

Index

Guided Reading Level: **B**
Guided Reading Leveling System is based on the guidelines recommended by Fountas and Pinnell.

Word Count: 41